L'ENFANT AIME
(A CHILD LOVES)

BY DARIUS MILHAUD
EDITED BY CAROLYN TRUE

CONTENTS

ISBN 978-1-4234-1525-1

HAL•LEONARD® CORPORATION
7777 W. BLUEMOUND RD. P.O. BOX 13819 MILWAUKEE, WI 53213

Visit Hal Leonard Online at
www.halleonard.com

ABOUT THE EDITOR

Hailed as "an artist with commanding technique, always at the service of the music and capable of taming any tigers the composer has unleashed" (Windeler, *San Antonio Express News*), Carolyn True is a pianist equally at home on the concert stage and in the teaching studio. A member of the music faculty of Trinity University, True teaches individual lessons, accompanying, piano ensemble, piano literature, piano pedagogy, and other related courses. She walks the delicate balance between teaching in San Antonio, giving workshops, master classes, seminars, and adjudicating and actively performing as soloist and chamber musician in the United States, Europe, and Asia. A compassionate and challenging professor, True is carrying on the family tradition. In 2000, True was recognized as the Texas Music Teachers Association's Collegiate Teacher of the Year and in 2010, she received the Dr. and Mrs. Z. T. Scott Faculty Fellowship from Trinity University in recognition of her outstanding abilities as a teacher and adviser.

Dr. True holds the prestigious Performer's Certificate and the D.M.A. degree from the Eastman School of Music, an M.M. from the University of Maryland-College Park, and the B.M. from the University of Central Missouri and was a prize winner in national and international competitions. She was also the recipient of a Rotary Foundation Scholarship for study at the Conservatoire National de la Musique in Lyon, France.

Her first solo CD, *Carolyn True 1*, features works of Ligeti, Bach/Brahms, Beethoven, and Bennett.

The editor thanks Daniel Milhaud.

DARIUS MILHAUD BIOGRAPHY

DARIUS MILHAUD (September 4, 1892 – June 22, 1974) begins his autobiography stating, "I am a Frenchman from Provence, and by religion a Jew." These two characteristics affected everything he wrote. Milhaud spent his childhood in Aix-en Provence, a city in the south of France full of mountains, beaches and the art of Paul Cezanne. He often walked in the country with his childhood friend Léo Latil. This love of his hometown and the French countryside traveled with him wherever he went. Milhaud reminisced about his favorite spots:

> "There was a big garden, divided in two by a path lined with chestnut trees...In certain years it became a rendezvous for sparrows; there they indulged in their mysterious games and made the air thrum with the flutter of their wings. I would read and work under an arbor of honeysuckle, looking out over the kitchen-gardens and the vines that clambered over the trellis...A little row of quince trees and hazel, above which towered a tall cypress, a pine, and two cedars, ran alongside the...road as far as the little entrance to our grounds. Every day I used to perch in the topmost branch of one of the cedars and watch for the carriage in which my father would drive home to lunch."

Even as a young boy, Milhaud was immersed in music. By age 17 Milhaud was a pupil at the Paris Conservatory, studying composition and violin. He was an extremely prolific composer. Early pieces included song settings of French poets (Jammes, Latil, Claudel, and others), a violin sonata, and a suite for solo piano. After graduation, Milhaud took a post at the Ministry of Foreign Affairs and shortly after was assigned to Paul Claudel as his secretary. Claudel was appointed the Minister to Brazil and took Milhaud with him. Several of Milhaud's most popular and enduring works were influenced by this two-year stint in Brazil, most notably the piano pieces *Saudades do Brasil* and the ever-popular *Scaramouche*.

On January 16, 1920 an article by Henri Collet spoke of two books by Rimsky and Cocteau and two groups of composers—Five Russians, Six French—and Eric Satie. "The Six," or in French, *Les Six*, were Darius Milhaud, Francis Poulenc, Arthur Honegger, George Auric, Germaine Tailleferre, and Louis Durey. According to Madeleine Milhaud, although the title grouping six diverse composers together was given in an artificial way, the label stuck and grew to be helpful. Les Six regularly gathered to share music, evening events and meals. Mme Milhaud spoke of the six:

> "Germaine was delightful—friendly, enthusiastic, disinterested...Honegger and Darius had been close friends at the Conservatoire. Although Arthur was attached to and influenced by German music, their differing tastes never came between them...Auric (was) precocious...His culture and vivacity were exceptional, and very different from various qualities of Francis, who was closer to Chabrier in spirit. Nobody could handle buffoonery quite like him!...Durey was the oldest member. And had been a good friend of Cocteau before the twenties."

In 1922 Milhaud traveled to London and had his first exposure to jazz. This had a profound influence on both his style and his manner of composition. Milhaud wrote:

> "The new music was extremely subtle in its use of timbre...The constant use of syncopation in the melody was of such contrapuntal freedom that it gave the impression of unregulated improvisation... I had the idea of using these timbres and rhythms...but first I had to penetrate more deeply into the arcane of this new musical form, whose technique still baffled me."

In the '20s and '30s Milhaud was extraordinarily busy. He taught, composed, and performed but grew aware of a heavy political presence gaining ground in France. By 1939, he realized that as a Jew, he and his family (his wife Madeleine and his son Daniel) were in a precarious position and they relocated to the United States. As teaching was an important part of Milhaud's life already, he happily took a full time teaching position at Mills College (Oakland, California) and in addition, became a fixture in several summer music festivals (Tanglewood, Aspen, and the Music Academy of the West in Santa Barbara, California). After the Second World War, Milhaud alternated teaching at the Paris Conservatory and Mills College. He juggled composing, performing, and teaching until his poor health forced him to retire in 1971. He died in Geneva in 1974.

PERFORMANCE NOTES AND MUSICAL CHARACTERISTICS

Milhaud's music is a study in variety, and *L'Enfant Aime* exhibits many of his characteristic compositional choices. Since these pieces are for and about children, one immediately hears singable tunes (although as with Chopin's melodies, these are some melodies with large, non-singable spans). Within each piece there are pitch and rhythmic motives that upon discovering, aid greatly in the learning, practicing, memorizing, and performing of these pieces. They exhibit popular idioms, often exploiting the inexorable rhythms of South America and the timbres and tempting harmonic language of folk songs and jazz. In close proximity, one will find polytonality and strong dissonance. Similar to Debussy, Milhaud's music is full of short motives linked together to produce long phrases, with complex harmonies. Counterpoint and imitation are evident in almost all of the five short pieces. Above all, it is the combination of harmonies (polytonality), textures, color, rhythmic activity, and musical lines that define his style. Even in his compositional life Milhaud embraced juxtapositions—writing a short set of pieces for children (L'Enfant Aime) while working a self-imposed compositional puzzle—two string quartets (Fourteenth and Fifteenth String Quartets) that would produce a third work (String Octet).

He wrote several works for younger students: *Touches noirs, touches blanches*, Op. 222 (1941), *Acceuil amical* Op. 326, 1944–5, *Une journee* Op. 269 (1946), and on November 30, 1948 while at Mills College—*L'enfant aime* (1948). *L'Enfant Aime* was premiered at the University of Wyoming in Laramie, Wyoming during a guest visit (1949).

Milhaud's set of pieces—*L'Enfant Aime* (A Child Loves)—is a musical reflection on facets of a child's life and loves. In the original manuscript, Milhaud marked an ellipsis ("...") following the title (*L'Enfant Aime...*), and separated the pieces by commas and a period after the last piece. The punctuation suggests that one can either play the pieces separately or as a group. Clearly, Milhaud (a father himself) knew and understood children and their ability to love many things at once!

In the manuscript, the titles appear in French and English:

L'Enfant Aime ...	A Child Loves...
1. les fleurs,	1. flowers,
2. les bonbons,	2. candy,
3. les jouets,	3. toys,
4. sa mère,	4. Mother,
5. la vie.	5. life.

PEDALING

Pedaling in French music is often tricky, but if one listens carefully, it is much less troublesome and quite wonderful to explore! In other words, listening for beauty of sound is the key. There is ample opportunity in these pieces to experiment with various levels of damper and una corda pedals, and even a few moments where one could use the sostenuto pedal for clarity. Milhaud left us few pedal indications, and none at all in *L'Enfant Aime*. All of the pedal indications are the editor's suggestions. When pedaling, several issues need to be addressed including (but certainly not limited to): the character of the piece, the color of the desired sound, the dryness or wetness of the sound, the carry-over of harmonies and/or melodic notes, and the function of rests, fermatas, and other durational indications. While much too often, pianists simply "put down the right foot" and take it off when the moment strikes them, one needs to be conscious of the variety of sounds possible by carefully chosen pedaling.

The pedal indications used in this edition are:

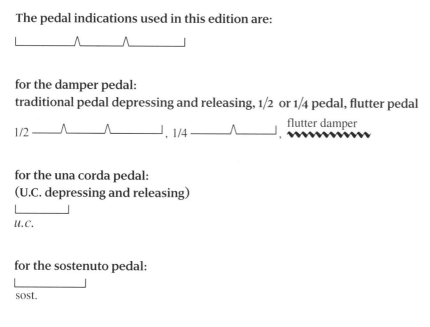

for the damper pedal:
traditional pedal depressing and releasing, 1/2 or 1/4 pedal, flutter pedal

for the una corda pedal:
(U.C. depressing and releasing)
u.c.

for the sostenuto pedal:
sost.

FINGERING

Fingering is as individual as hands are different. When choosing fingerings, one needs to address the desires of the composer (length and dynamic of note patterns, articulation, other expressive elements), phrasing, geography of the keyboard, and natural and efficient physical motions produced by understanding the parameters of the individual hand—length of fingers, breadth of expanse, girth of the fingers and the palm. The fingerings for this edition are merely suggestions (the editor's are in italics, the composer's are in normal text). As with pedaling, pianists must spend time exploring fingering options and coming to a conscious decision for each passage. In this way, the musical goals will always be first and foremost.

PHRASES

Milhaud left numerous articulation marks, grouping pitches into short units. Looking closely one finds two levels of natural phrases in *L'Enfant Aime*—the macro (longer phrases of 8–10 bars in length) and the micro (2–4 measure units). Often they are clearly delineated by rests, expressive marks, harmonies, or longer note values, but more often than not the phrases overlap. The editor has marked suggested macro-phrase lifts with breath marks.

PRACTICE AND PERFORMANCE SUGGESTIONS

1. LES FLEURS

This carefree little piece exploits the typical 6/8 rhythmic pattern of quarter-eighth. Active listening will match the sound decay from the quarter note to the eighth and will allow one to sing the line. Singing the melodic line before playing it will help achieve the natural, but lengthy macro-phrases (mm.1–10, 11–23, 24–28, 29–42). Much like singing a Chopin melodic line you will need to adjust your octave for physical comfort! *Les fleurs* shifts effortlessly from two main pulses to three (hemiola). Careful metronome practice will keep the pulse steady and help to avoid the natural forward motion (for example mm.15–20). The suggested fingerings will allow for clear articulation and ease of motion throughout the phrases. Milhaud adds a white note cluster in both hands at the final cadence. It is played and some of the pitches are released to leave a dominant triad which resolves (through a rest) to the C Major tonic triad.

2. LES BONBONS

Les bonbons is indeed a tasty little treat! Although without a key signature, it is clearly in G Major. The short two-measure motive in the right-hand melody (mm. 1–2) forms the basis of the entire work. Perhaps Milhaud was depicting morsels of candy in one small handful—each slightly different than the other, but connected by recipe and shape? Eat and savor these morsels slowly by practicing the opening two measures and all of the different incarnations (right hand: mm. 9–10, 15–16, 36–37; left hand: mm. 3–4, 17–18, and 38–39). Notice how Milhaud changed each through intervallic expansion or contraction.

3. LES JOUETS

Milhaud must have had a wonderful nursery full of different toys. One hears a rocking horse, sees a top spinning, all in a room certainly big enough for running! These different "toys" make for rapid changes of texture and technical challenges. Within the first phrase the right hand must play perfect fifths with an upper neighbor pattern in the top voice, a galloping two-note motive moving up and back with C5 as the fulcrum, and a Bb Major scale starting on A4 and ending on C6. Practice each gesture separately with all of the similar passages to find the natural gesture of fingers, wrist, and arm. After each gesture can be accomplished with ease, re-connect them into one long phrase. Notice how carefully Milhaud marks note lengths (for example mm1–3 left-hand quarter note to eighth-note rest opposite dotted quarter note in the right-hand thumb). These slight but important differences will make the toys come alive!

4. SA MÈRE

This is the slowest piece of the group and the only one that changes meter (from 4/4 to 2/4 in m17). A "maman" (mother) motive of a descending third recurs throughout *sa mère*. See how many you can find (look for both ascending and descending thirds). There are two passages of tricky ascending parallel fourths (mm. 7–9 and 34–35). Practice this passage hands alone, playing the top voice legato and the bottom voice staccato. Repeated blocked seconds pervade the piece. Keep them light and graceful under the melody by keeping your wrist flexible and supple. Using the sostenuto pedal in this movement will help both define the voices and allow the use of the damper to produce a warm, beautiful sound.

5. LA VIE

In *la vie* the texture moves between a right-hand melody with a single note left-hand accompaniment, to a right-hand melody with a blocked three-note accompaniment, to brassy second inversion triads. During mm.11–13 Milhaud obscures the regular metric pulse of 2/2, choosing instead to group pulses into three quarter-note units. The harmony of the third beat of each unit is slightly different. Listen to each final chord (m11, A Major, m12 G Major, m 13 F Major, and lastly E7) and choose tonal colors that communicate the difference in harmony. In mm. 16–23 the accents define the right-hand meter as 2/2 and the left hand as 3/4. This same polymeter also occurs in mm. 32–34 and mm. 48–53. Practice each of these polymeter sections hands alone to stay true to the impulses and accents. Then practice hands together, taking care to hear both meters working simultaneously.

RESOURCES

Nichols, Roger. *Conversations with Madeline Milhaud*. England: Faber and Faber Limited, 1996.

Milhaud, Darius. *Notes without Music*. New York: Alfred A. Knopf, Da Capo Press Reprint Edition, 1952, 53.

Kelly, Barbara L. *Tradition and Style in the Works of Darius Milhaud 1912–1939*. Burlington, VT: Ashgate Publishing Co., 2003.

to nicole leduc

les fleurs
flowers

By Darius Milhaud

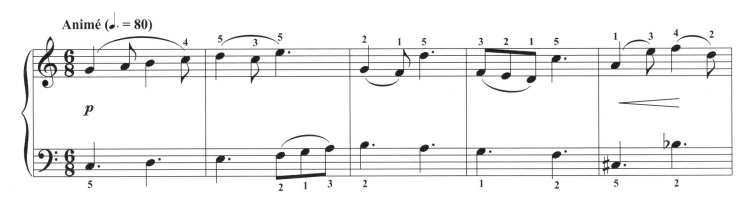

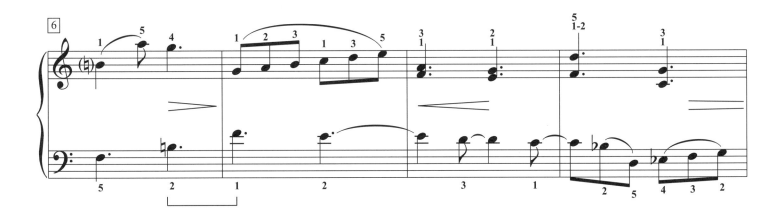

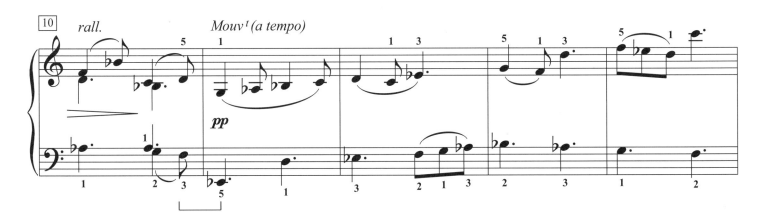

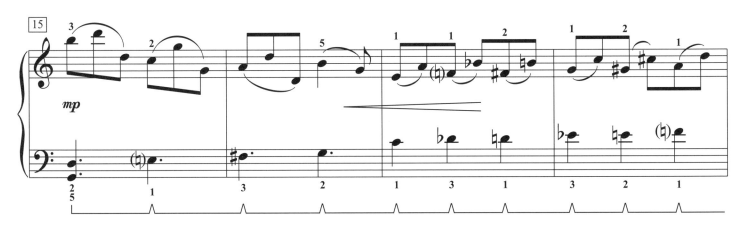

10

to edmonde wilson

les bonbons
candy

By Darius Milhaud

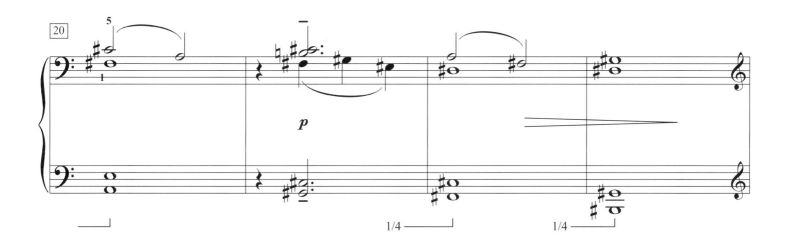

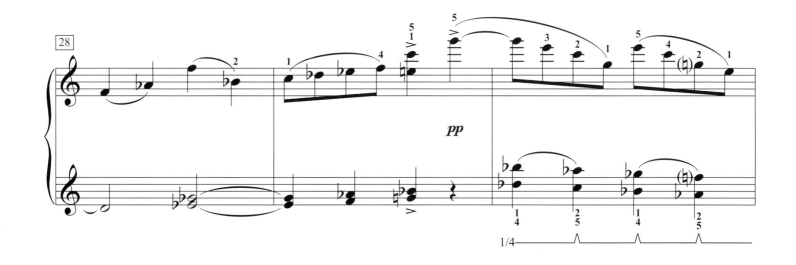

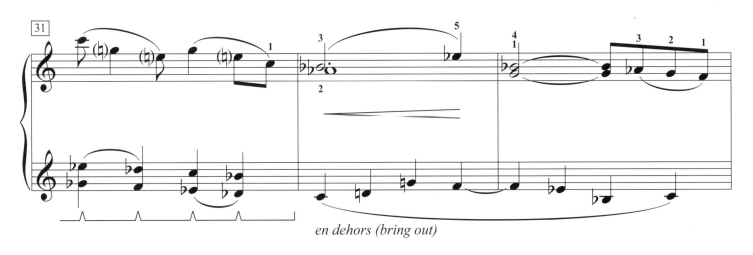

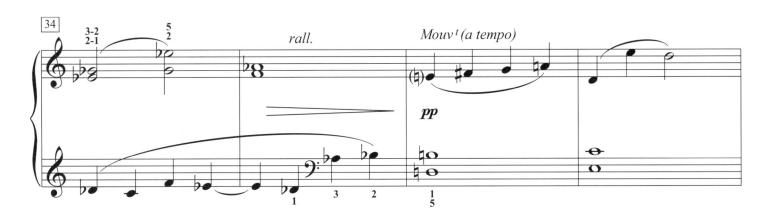

en dehors (bring out)

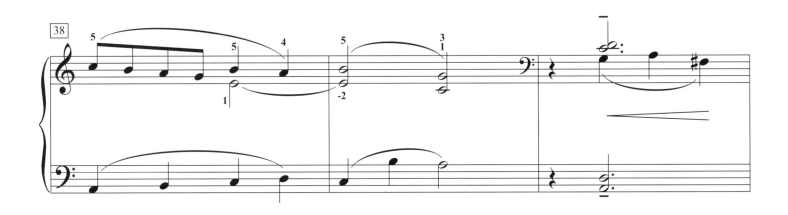

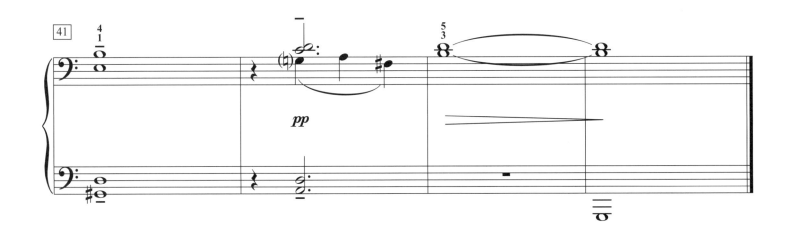

to dominique bailey

les jouets
toys

By Darius Milhaud

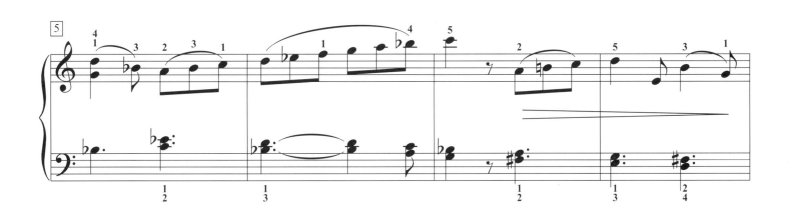

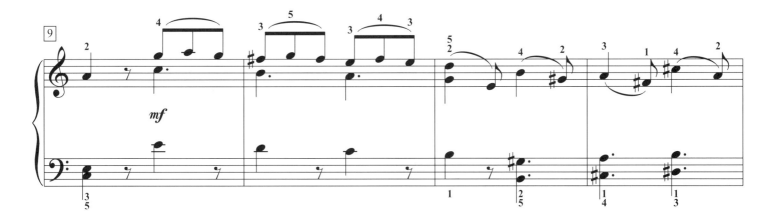

to niccolo daniele rieti

sa mère
mother

By Darius Milhaud

pedal as before

This page has been left blank to facilitate page turns.

to catherine vellay

la vie

life

By Darius Milhaud

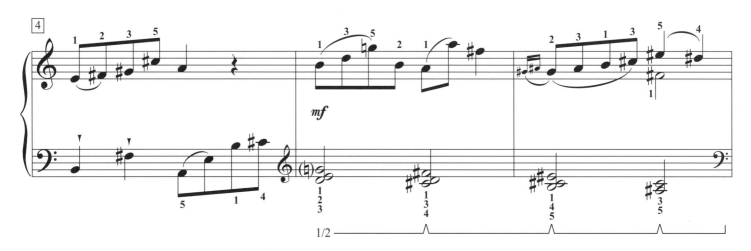

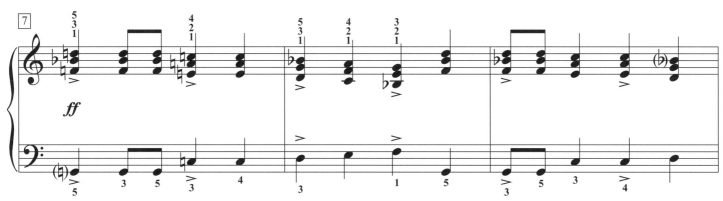